THE TRADESMEN AND GENTRY OF TAMWORTH

A GLIMPSE OF THE STAFFORDSHIRE TOWN IN 1818 AND 1864

FROM EXTRACTS OF TRADE DIRECTORIES.

BY GEOFFREY HUGH LINDOP

First published by Mercianotes 2016

Published by
Mercianotes,
Brackenrigg
Wigton,
Cumbria
CA7 5AQ

ISBN: 978-1535358798

www.mercianotes.com

Email: enquiries@mercianotes.com

A

Adams George, stationer, Silver street Resident in 1864

Adams James, Old Star inn, Gungate street Resident in 1864

Adams Robert, linendraper, Silver street Resident in 1864

Adams William, butcher, Market place Resident in 1864

Adcock Mr. William, Lady bank Resident in 1864

Adcock William, miller, Castle mills Resident in 1864

Addison Christopher, news agent, Silver street Resident in 1864

Ackroyd Jeremiah, Tailor and draper, Silver street Resident in 1818

Aitken Peter, travelling draper, Aldergate street Resident in 1864

Aldridge Samuel, currier and leather cutter, Church street Resident in 1864

Alldritt James, cattle castrator, Bolebridge street Resident in 1818

Alldritt Joseph, boot and shoemaker, Bole Bridge street Resident in 1818

Allen Hannah, dealer in tobacco and confectionary, Cole hill Resident in 1818

Allen James, gardener, Cole hill Resident in 1818

Allen James, blacksmith & shopkeeper, Kettlebrook Resident in 1864

Allen James, hairdresser & glass & china warehouse, Market street Resident in 1864

Allen Sarah, victulier, Star, Cole hill Resident in 1818

Allen Thomas, engraver to callico printers, Peel street Resident in 1818

Allen Thomas, shopkeeper, Gungate street Resident in 1864

Tamworth as described in 1864

Tamworth is so situated that the boundary line of the counties of Warwick and Stafford passes through the middle of the town. It is in the hundred of South Offlow and of Hemlingford, Tamworth poor law union and deanery, diocese of Lichfield, and archeaconry of Stafford. It is a borough, returning two members to Parliament, a municipality, railway station and union town. Tamworth has a considerable market for corn. It is situated in an undulating country, well watered by excellent springs, as well as the two rivers Tame and Tinker, which unite at the foot of the old castle.

(Continued on page 5)

Allen William, seedsman, Bolebridge street Resident in 1864

Allport Mr. Richard, cutler, Church street Resident in 1818
Allport Mr. Richard, Lichfield street Resident in 1864

Allsop Benjamin,, market gardener, Gungate street Resident in 1864

Allsop Thomas, gardener, Lichfield Street Resident in 1818

Allsop Thomas, higgler, Bole Street Resident in 1818

Allsop Samuel, fishmonger, Bolebridge street Resident in 1864

Anderson Rev. William, M.A. [curate of Fazeley], Lichfield street Resident in 1864

Argyle of Willington & Argyle, solicitors, & clerks to trustees of Tamworth turnpike roads, Cole hill Resident in 1864

Argyle Thomas esq., Cole hill Resident in 1864

Arnold David Joseph & Thomas, Ale & porter brewers, Castle brewery Resident in 1864

Arnold Mrs., Ladybridge bank Resident in 1864

Arnold Mr. Joseph, Tailor, Lichfield Street Resident in 1818

Arnold Mr. Joseph, Tailor, Market Place Resident in 1818

Arnold Mr. Joseph, The Lees Resident in 1864

Arnold Mr. Samuel, Albert road Resident in 1864

Arnold Mr. Thomas, Maltster and brickmaker, Lichfield street Resident in 1818
Arnold Mr. Thomas, Lichfield street Resident in 1864

Arnold Mr. William, Albert road Resident in 1864

Arnold William, gardener, Glascote Resident in 1864

Ashley Alfred, working cutler &c. Church street Resident in 1864

Ashwood William, bootmaker, Church street Resident in 1864

Atkin Maria (Miss), milliner & dressmaker, Gungate street Resident in 1864

Atkins Anne, seminary for young ladies, George street Resident in 1818

Atkins James, pig dealer, Lichfield street Resident in 1818

Atkins (the Misses), dressmakers, Lichfield street Resident in 1864

B

Bailey Charles, hairdresser, George street Resident in 1864

Bailey Edwin, sen. gardener & seedsman, Bolebridge street Resident in 1864

Bailey Edwin, jun. brazier &china & glass dealer, George st Resident in 1864

Bailey John, farmer, Lichfield street Resident in 1818

Bailey John, ironmonger, Market street Resident in 1864

Bailey Joshua, hosier and woolcomber, Bole bridge street Resident in 1818

Baker Edward, surgeon, Church street Resident in 1818

Baker Richard, watch and clock maker, bookseller and stationer, Market street Resident in 1818

Baker Thomas, pork butcher, George street Resident in 1864

Baker Thomas, sign painter, Gungate street Resident in 1864

Baldwin John, baker & shopkeeper, Bolebridge street Resident in 1864

Ballard James, Swan, Bolebridge street Resident in 1864

Ballard William Henry, butcher, Bolebridge street Resident in 1864

Bamford Mrs , Bolehall house Resident in 1864

Barber John Hubbard, shoemaker, Church street Resident in 1864

Barber John boot and shoemaker, College lane Resident in 1818

Barber Thomas,senior, higgler, Gungate street Resident in 1818

Barlow George, chimney sweeper, Gungate stree: Resident in 1864

Barlow Joseph, tailor, Church lane Resident in 1818

Barraclough Samuel, shoemaker & news agent, Lit.Market st Resident in 1864

Barratt L.R.A, gentlewoman, Gungate street Resident in 1818

Barratt Richard, linen and woolen draper, straw hat manufacturer Silver street Resident in 1818

Barratt Richard, draper, Market street Resident in 1864

(Continued from page 3)

Commons

There are two commons or moors, the Staffordshire and Warwickshire moors, upon which the inhabitants of ancient messuages have common rights each for one head of cattle : the soil in the immediate neighbourhood of the town is exceedingly rich and fertile: there are very valuable mines of coal fire clay, and blue and red brick clay, extensively worked: Market gardening is carried on to a very great extent, considerable supplies being sent to Birmingham. There is a Farmers' club, and a Horticultural society. There are two manufactories for small wares, and two considerable paper manufactories. The market is held on Saturday.

(Continued on page 8)

Barton J. C. , King's Arms Inn, Market street Resident in 1818

Bassett George, saddler and harness maker, Bole bridge street Resident in 1818

Bassford Thomas, grocer, Glascote Resident in 1864

Batchelor Tom, inspector of police on railways, Victoria rd Resident in 1864

Batchelor William, gardener. Church street Resident in 1818

Bates John, tailor, Litchfield street Resident in 1864

Baynard James, agent to the Kettlebrook colliery, George st and agent for trustees of the late John Dumolo Resident in 1864

Baynard Mr. James, George street Resident in 1864

Beach Thomas, butcher, Bole bridge street Resident in 1818

Beard Charles, printer, Market place Resident in 1864

Beard Joseph, letter-press printer and book binder, Market street Resident in 1818

Beard Thomas, brick maker and maltster, Gungate street Resident in 1818

Beard William, brick maker and maltster, Church street Resident in 1818

Beckett William, butcher, Church street Resident in 1864

Beer Richard, gentleman, Lichfield street Resident in 1818

Bennet Priscillia (Mrs), gentlewoman, Lichfield street Resident in 1818

Bennet Richard, joiner and builder, Eldergate street Resident in 1818

Bennet Thomas, surgeon, Lichfield street Resident in 1818

Best Edward, coal proprietor, Park and Kettlebrook Colliery in 1818

Biddle Richard, cabinet maker & upholsterer, Lichfield st Resident in 1864

Biddle Robert, Queen's Head, Lichfield street Resident in 1864

Biddle William, Malt Shovel, Lichfield street Resident in 1864

Bindley Thomas, fell monger and oil lether dresser, George street< Resident in 1818

Bindley William senior, gentleman, Lichfield street Resident in 1818

Bindley William, tallow chandler, flax dresser, rope maker etc, George street< Resident in 1818

Bindley William, auctioneer, grocer, tallow chandler & rope & twine manufacturer, George street Resident in 1864

Birch James, cooper, George street Resident in 1818

Birch Mrs., Albert road Resident in 1864

Bircher Alfred, shoeing smith, Bolebridge street Resident in 1864

Bird Richard, surgeon, George street Resident in 1818

Bird Sarah (Mrs.), lodging house, Albert road Resident in 1864

Blackwell William porter near Lichfield street Resident in 1818

Blick the Rev. Francis vicar of Tamworth Mill field Resident in 1818

Blood Thomas butcher and farmer, Market street Resident in 1818

Blood William esq., George street Resident in 1864

Blount John, butcher, Gungate street Resident in 1864

Blow John, carpenter, Amington Resident in 1864

Blow Joshua, watchmaker, Market street Resident in 1864

Blower Samuel, tailor, Bolebridge street Resident in 1864

Bodell Thomas hatter, Bolebridge street Resident in 1818

Bothams John jpiner and shopkeeper, Gungate street Resident in 1818

Bourne Mrs., Aldergate street Resident in 1864

Bourne Miss Mary, gentlewoman, Cole street Resident in 1818

Boyes William, plumber &c. Gungate street Resident in 1864

Bradbury Mr. Isaac, Albert road Resident in 1864

Bradgate Mrs Sarah, gentlewoman, Lichfield street Resident in 1818

Bradley Joseph, shopkeeper, Amington Resident in 1864

Brain John, joiner and carpenter, Gungate street Resident in 1818

Bramall Thomas esq., J.P. Lichfield st Resident in 1864

Brant Charles, joiner and builder, Gungate street Resident in 1818

Bridgewood Charles, victualler, White Horse Inn, Lichfield street Resident in 1818

Britt William, hairdresser, Cole hill Resident in 1864

Brittain Thomas, stone and marble mason, and bricklayer Eldergate street Resident in 1818

Broster M.T., victualler, King's Head, Market street Resident in 1818

Broster William, carter, Church street Resident in 1818

Brown Francis, grocer, Bolebridge street Resident in 1818

Brown John, plumber & glazier, Aldergate street Resident in 1864

Brown Joseph, straw hat manufacturer, Church street Resident in 1818

Brown Mrs., gentlewoman, Church street Resident in 1818

Buck James, gardener and seedsman, Market street Resident in 1818

Buckerfield John, farmer, George street Resident in 1864

Buckerfield Thomas, hat manufacturer, George street Resident in 1818

Bull Edward Hames, plumber, Church street Resident in 1864

Bullers Mrs., Albert road Resident in 1864

Burdekin Rev. Jas. [curate], Victoria rd Resident in 1864

Burgess Rev. Thomas [Independent], Aldergate street Resident in 1864

Burkitt Joseph, blacksmith, Gungate street Resident in 1818

Burton John, boot and shoemaker, Silver street Resident in 1818

Butler John, gentleman, Church street Resident in 1818

Butler John, ironmonger and whitesmith, Church street Resident in 1818

Butler Mary (Mrs.), ironmonger, Market street Resident in 1864

Butler Miss, Lichfield street Resident in 1864

Butler & Bullock (Misses), ladies' boarding school, Lichfield st Resident in 1864

Butterworth John, manager of the Castle Lint mills Resident in 1864

Byng Rev. John, dissenting minister, Cole hill Resident in 1818

Byng Thomas, grocer and druggist, Market place Resident in 1818

C

Caditel David, gentleman, Bole bridge street Resident in 1818

Camp James, hairdresser, Church street Resident in 1864

Canning Charles esq., Glascote Resident in 1864

Capewell James, gardener, Gungate street Resident in 1864

Capewell John, boot & shoe maker, George street Resident in 1864

Carter Joseph, boot and shoemaker, George street Resident in 1818

Carter Joseph, shoemaker, Bolebridge street Resident in 1864

Carter Thomas, shoemaker, George street Resident in 1864

(Continued from page 5)

Almshouses
Guy's Almshouses were established by the celebrated Guy, founder of the hospital in London, and who was member for Tamworth when he built and endowed the almshouses: he also gave the old Town Hall, to which two rooms were added by the first Sir Robert Peel.

(Continued on page 12)

Cawley Joseph, tailor, Aldergate street Resident in 1864

Chater Mary Ann (Miss), school teacher, Aldergate street Resident in 1864

Chamberlain Mrs MAry, gentlewoman, Bole bridge street Resident in 1818

Chambley William, clock maker, Lady bridge bank Resident in 1818

Champion Thomas, shoemaker, near Lichfield street Resident in 1818

Chattaway John, butcher, Church street Resident in 1818

Chatterton John, druggist & grocer, Market street Resident in 1864

Cheshire Mrs., Lichfield street Resident in 1864

Clamp Thomas, beer retailer, Gungate street Resident in 1864

Clark James, boot and shoemaker, Church street Resident in 1818

Clark Misses, Gungate street Resident in 1864

Clarke William, stone mason and painter, Gungate street Resident in 1818

Clarke William, bookbinder, Gungate street Resident in 1818

Clarson Abel, draper, Market place Resident in 1864

Clarson Charles, builder, Aldergate street Resident in 1864

Clarson Joseph Henry, bricklayer, Albert road Resident in 1864

Clarson Mrs., Lichfield street Resident in 1864

Clement Richard, boot and shoemaker, Bole bridge street Resident in 1818

Clements Richard, professor. of music, tuner, photographic artist & organist at Drayton church, Church street Resident in 1864

Cleminshaw John, schoolmaster, Gungate street Resident in 1818

Coleman Thomas, victualler, Rose and Crown Inn, Market street Resident in 1818

Collingwood Thomas, boot and shoemaker, George street Resident in 1818

Collins Thomas, baker and flour dealer, Lichfield street Resident in 1818

Collins William, miller, Lichfield street Resident in 1818

Cooke Mr. William, Albert road Resident in 1864

Cooke Thomas & Co. wholesale clothiers, Lichfield street Resident in 1864

Cooper James, plumber & glazier, Market street Resident in 1864

Cooper Sarah (Mrs.), toy dealer, Market street Resident in 1864

Cooper Thomas, watch and clock maker, George street Resident in 1818

Cope Thomas, butcher, Lichfield street Resident in 1818

Cope Thomas, higgler, Gungate street Resident in 1818

Coton John, game dealer, Bolebridge street Resident in 1864

Coton John, weighing machine, Kettlebrook wharf and agent for trustees of the late John Dumolo coal owner & merchant Resident in 1864

Coton Susannah (Mrs.), Cole hill Resident in 1818

Coton Thomas, wine and brandy merchant, and brick maker, George street Resident in 1818

Cotton Richard, letter-press printer and auctioneer, Church street Resident in 1818

Cotton Thomas, joiner, Lichfield street Resident in 1818

Coulson William Thomas, haberdasher, Church street Resident in 1864

Crowley Eliza,(Mrs.), gentlewoman, Cole hill Resident in 1818

Cox Edward, shoe warehouse, George street Resident in 1864

Cox Hannah, (Mrs.), Lichfield street Resident in 1818

Cox James, boot and shoe maker, Bole bridge street Resident in 1818

Cox Francis, druggist and grocer, George street Resident in 1818

Cox Thomas, (Mr.), Albert road Resident in 1864

Cox William, surgeon, Lichfield street Resident in 1818

Cox & Co. wine & spirit merchants, Market place Resident in 1864

Coxon William, baker and flour dealer, Church street Resident in 1818

Crocket Richard, gardener, Bolebridge street Resident in 1864

D

Daff William, traveller, Bole bridge street Resident in 1818

Dale Selina (Mrs.), milliner, Aldergate street Resident in 1864

Dale Susannah, hair dresser, George street Resident in 1818

Davis William, Gate inn, Amington Resident in 1864

Davis William, nail manufacturer, Bole bridge street Resident in 1818

Dawes Miss Mary, gentlewoman, Church street Resident in 1818

Day Philip, grocer and flour dealer, Church street Resident in 1818

Deakin Jane (Mrs.), White Horse, Lichfield street Resident in 1864

Dennant Abraham, grocer and draper, Church street Resident in 1818

Dewsbury David, plumber and glazier, Church street Resident in 1818

Dimbleby David, confectioner, Church street Resident in 1864

Dissenting Meeting House, Cole hill Resident in 1818

Dove Richard Thackery, butcher, Litchfield street Resident in 1864

Dovey John, boot & shoe maker, Church street Resident in 1864

Downes Rev. S, master of the free Grammar School, Gungate street Resident in 1818

Drake Richard, boot and shoemaker, George street Resident in 1818

Drake Thomas, shoemaker, Church street Resident in 1818

Dudley John, butcher, Bole bridge street Resident in 1818

Dudley Mary, victualler, Coffee Pot, George street Resident in 1818

Duffy James, brazier and tin plate worker, Market street Resident in 1818

Duffy Mrs., Victoria road Resident in 1864

Dumolo John coal owner & merchant ((trustees of the late James Baynard, agent), Kettlebrook wharf; & (John Coton, agent) Fazeley wharf, Fazeley Resident in 1864

Dumolo Thomas, land surveyor & land & mining agent, Aldergate street Resident in 1864

Dyer Alfred, confectioner, Silver street Resident in 1864

E

Earnshaw James, Millwright, Greengate street Resident in 1818

Earp John, clothier, George street Resident in 1864

Eaton Emma (Miss), shoe warehouse, Market street Resident in 1864

Eaton George, Tamworth Arms, & soda water manufacturer, Market street Resident in 1864

Eaton Judith (Mrs.), Anchor, Glascote Resident in 1864

Eaton Sarah Ann (Mrs.), ginger beer maker, Aldergate st Resident in 1864

Eaves Thomas, gardener, Lichfield street Resident in 1818

Edden Thomas, corn and flour dealer, Market place Resident in 1818

Edwards Leonard, Globe, Gungate street Resident in 1864

Edwards Mark, provision dealer, Market street Resident in 1864

Edwards Wood William esq., Tamworth castle Resident in 1864

Endsor Thomas, plumber, glazier and sign painter, Silver street Resident in 1818

Endsor William, white and blacksmith, College lane street Resident in 1818

Ensor Henry, farmer, Warren house, Amington Resident in 1864

Ensor Joseph, tailor, Bolebridge street Resident in 1864

Ensor Mary (Mrs.), staymaker, Bolebridge street Resident in 1864

Ensor Thomas, farmer, Amington Resident in 1864

Entwistle Sergeant Major, Bolehall Resident in 1864

Evans Evan, officer of excise, Bole bridge street Resident in 1818

Evans John, auctioneer, George street Resident in 1818

Evans Mr. John, Albert road Resident in 1864

F

Fairbrother Ann (Miss), milliner etc. St. .John's place, Aldergate street Resident in 1864

Fairfield William, Golden Cup, Gungate street Resident in 1864

Famath William, shopkeeper, Bolebridge street Resident in 1864

Farmer Joseph, grocer and druggist, Bole bridge street Resident in 1818

Felthouse Charles, druggist & grocer, Market place Resident in 1864

Felthouse Henry & John, curriers & leather sellers, Church st Resident in 1864

Fenton James, watch and clock maker , Market street Resident in 1818

Fenton Thomas, hair dresser, Silver street Resident in 1818

Fielding Joseph, shopkeeper, Amington Resident in 1864

Fisher Charles & Co. paper makers, Kettlebrook mills Resident in 1864

Fletcher William, fish monger, Market street Resident in 1818

Forman George, shoemaker, Market street Resident in 1864

Foster Mrs., Ellen, Victoria road Resident in 1864

Foster William, joiner and cabinet maker, Church street Resident in 1818

Foulkes Thomas, Horse & Jockey, Church street Resident in 1864

Found William, boot & shoe maker, George street Resident in 1864

(Continued from page 8)

Castle
The castle, which was long the royal residence of our Saxon kings, and added to by Queen Ethelfleda, was the seat of the Marmions, given to them by William the Conqueror; and here, on its walls and foundations, is a noble castellated mansion of the Marquis Townshend, the representative of the Marmions ; the castle is now the residence of W. Edwards Wood, Esq., and contains articles of virtu and an extensive collection of valuable paintings.

(Continued on page 17)

Fowler W.J. & J., cotton spinners, meal men, paper makers, oil crushers and coal merchants, Alder Mills Resident in 1818

Fox Francis, cooper, George street Resident in 1864

Francis Mr. John, Lichfield street Resident in 1864

Frearson Mr. Samuel, Glascote Resident in 1864

Freeman John, Esq, Cole hill Resident in 1818

Freeman Mr. William, Bolebridge street Resident in 1864

Freeman R.F., gentleman, Church street Resident in 1818

Freeman Samuel, farmer, malster and corn dealer, George street Resident in 1818

Freeman Thomas, butcher, Church street Resident in 1818

Freeman William, victualler, Old Swan, Bole bridge street Resident in 1818

Freer John wood turner and chair maker, George street Resident in 1818

Fulleylove George, tailor, Church street Resident in 1864

G

Gadsby John, schoolmaster, Albert road Resident in 1864

Gibbs Mr. John, Glascote Resident in 1864

Gibbs & Canning, manufacturers of sewerage pipes, Glascote Clay works Resident in 1864

Gilbert Arthur; tailor, Lichfield street Resident in 1864

Glover Charles, tailor and habit maker, Gungate street Resident in 1818

Gilbert Charles, horse dealer, Albert road Resident in 1864

Gilbert William, tailor and draper, Lichfield street Resident in 1818

Glover Samuel, grocer, Silver street Resident in 1818

Glover Samuel, grocer, Silver street Resident in 1864

Godderidge James, Bricklayers Arms, George street Resident in 1864

Godderidge Fhoebe (Mrs.), Lamb, Bolehall Resident in 1864

Godderidge William, shoemaker, Lichfield street Resident in 1864

Godderidge. George, cabinet maker, Bolehall Resident in 1864

Goodwin Charles, Star, Gungate street Resident in 1864

Grattidge Daniel. grocer, Gungate street Resident in 1864

Greaves John Twelch, professor of music, Albert road Resident in 1864

Green Richard, woolstapler, Church street Resident in 1818

Green Robert, cooper Church lane Resident in 1864

Grimley William, seedsman, Bolebridge street Resident in 1864

Gurney Rev. John Langton [curate], Colehill Resident in 1864

H

Haddon John, wheelwright, Church street Resident in 1818

Hall James, baker and flour dealer, Gungate street Resident in 1818

Hall John (Mr.), George street Resident in 1864

Hall John, grocer, tallow chandler, rope maker and flax dresser, George street Resident in 1818

Hall John, wheelwright, Lichfield steet Resident in 1818

Hallum Joseph, paper maker, Church street Resident in 1818

Halstead Mary (Mrs), gentlewoman, Church street Resident in 1818

Hamel Alfred & Egbert, small ware manufacturers, Bolehall mill Resident in 1864

Hamel Bruno, french teacher, wholsale glass, china and earthenware dealer George street Resident in 1818

Hamel Etienne (Mr.), Bolebridge street Resident in 1864

Hamel Etienne Bruno esq., J.P. Millfield house Resident in 1864

Hamel Etienne Bruno & Son, tape & small ware manufacturers, Bolebridge factory Resident in 1864

Hand James, farmer, Amington Old hall Resident in 1864

Hanson Samuel, grocer, druggist & hop merchant, Market st Resident in 1864

Harding Alexander, pattern drawer, New Row, Lichfield street Resident in 1818

Harding and Co, Tamworth Old Bank, George street Resident in 1818

Harding Charles esq., Bolehall Resident in 1864

Harding Miss, Lichfield street Resident in 1864

Hardy John, baker and flour dealer, Church street Resident in 1818

Hare Abraham, joiner, Lichfield street Resident in 1818

Hare Harriot & Emma (Misses), Albert rd Resident in 1864

Hare Henry, plumber &c. Market street Resident in 1864

Hare Isaac (junior), linen and woollen draper, Market place Resident in 1818

Hare Isaac (senior), gentleman, Market place Resident in 1818

Harper Daniel, gentleman, George street Resident in 1818

Harper Hannah (Mrs.), gentlewoman, George street Resident in 1818

Harris Anne, milliner and dressmaker, Bolebridge street Resident in 1818

Harris Thomas, joiner and cabinet maker,and upholsterer Bolebridge street Resident in 1818

Harris William, fishmonger and carrier, Lichfield street Resident in 1818

Harrison Daniel, sen. butcher, Lichfield street Resident in 1864

Harrison of Perrins & Harrison, coal owners & coal merchants, Kettlebrook wharf Resident in 1864

Hastilow Charles, farmer, Amington Resident in 1864

Hastilow James, farmer, Ashlands, Amington Resident in 1864

Hastilow James, shopkeeper, Bolebridge street Resident in 1864

Hastilow James, victualler, Old White Lion, Bolebridge street Resident in 1818

Hastilow John, Jolly Button Turner, Bolebridge street Resident in 1864

Hastilow John, sen. shopkeeper, Gungate street Resident in 1864

Hastilow John, shoemaker and cow-keeper, Bolebridge street Resident in 1818

Hastilow William, wheelwright, Gungate street. Resident in 1864

Hatton Henry, butcher, Church street Resident in 1864

Hawke William, stone and marble mason, Gungate street Resident in 1818

Hawkins Charles, victualler, Three Tuns Lichfield street Resident in 1818

Hawksford Richard, tailor, Church street Resident in 1818

Hawksworth and Bindley, milliners and dress makers, Market Place Resident in 1818

Hawksworth Hannah, Bookseller, stationer, tea dealer, confectioner etc, Market Place Resident in 1818

Haywood John, farmer, King street Resident in 1818

Heath (Mrs.), Cole hill Resident in 1864

Heath Joseph, corn miller, Cole Hill Resident in 1818

Henshaw John, tailor and habir maker, Lichfield street Resident in 1818

Hewitt Barbara (Mrs.), gentlewoman, Lichfield street Resident in 1818

Higginson Sarah, schoolmistress, Gungate street Resident in 1818

Hill (Miss), Victoria road Resident in 1864

Hill John (Mr.), Lady bank Resident in 1864

Hill John, Savings Bank actuary, Lady bank Resident in 1864

Hill Thomas, hosier, etc., Cole Hill Resident in 1818

Hitches Charles, Old Red Lion, Bolebridge street Resident in 1864

Hodgkinson Thomas, market gardener, Gungate street Resident in 1864

Holden (Mrs.), Aldergate street Resident in 1864

Holloway Gilbert, basket maker, Church street Resident in 1818

Holloway William, skinner, Church street Resident in 1818

Holloway William, turner & chair maker, Gungate street Resident in 1864

Holmes Elizabeth (Mrs.), Lichfield street Resident in 1818

Holmes Thomas, solicitor, Lichfield street Resident in 1818

Holyoake James, blacksmith, Gungate street Resident in 1864

Hopkins Joseph, blacksmith, Lichfield street Resident in 1818

Horton Ann (Mrs.), milliner, Albert road Resident in 1864

Hunter Charles, silversmith, ironmonger and agent to the Phoenix Fire Office, Market street Resident in 1818

Hunter David, Hair dresser and perfumer, Church street Resident in 1818

Hunter Elizabeth (Mrs.), gentlewoman, George street Resident in 1818

Hunter Francis, plumber & glazier, Cole hill Resident in 1864

Hunter James, gardener, Gungate street Resident in 1818

Hunter James, tailor, Church street Resident in 1818

Hunter John, bricklayer, Lichfield street Resident in 1818

Hunter John, calico printer, Bole Bridge street Resident in 1818

Hunter John, cotton ball manufacturer, Market street Resident in 1818

Hunter William, joiner, Lichfield street Resident in 1818

Huntsworth John, inland revenue officer, Lichfield' street Resident in 1864

I

Ison John, whitesmith, Gungate street Resident in 1864

Ison William, blacksmith, Lichfield street Resident in 1818

Ison William, haberdasher, George street Resident in 1864

J

Jackson Edward, block printer, College lane Resident in 1818

Jackson Jefcoat Samuel, victualler and flour dealer, Old Holly Bush, Lichfield street Resident in 1818

Jackson Samuel, boot & shoe maker, Lichfield street Resident in 1864

Jackson William, confectioner, baker and flour dealer, Silver street Resident in 1818

Jackson William, ostler, King street Resident in 1818

Jennings John Lea, wholesale grocer & druggist, Market place Resident in 1864

Jennings Mr. John, The Paddock Resident in 1864

Jennings Thomas, shoemaker, Church lane Resident in 1818

Johnson (Miss.), seminary for young ladies, Church street Resident in 1818

Johnson William, victualler Waggon and Horses, George street Resident in 1818

Jones & Son, shopkeepers, Bolebridge street Resident in 1864

Jones Edward, boot and shoemaker and earthenware manufacturer, Bole bridge street Resident in 1818

Jones Edward, cabinet maker and upholsterer, Silver street Resident in 1818

Jones Elizabeth, schoolmistress, Church street Resident in 1818

Jones Henry and Thomas, maltsters, George street Resident in 1818

Jones Henry, carpet weaver, College lane Resident in 1818

Jones Rev. Charles [curate], Cole hill Resident in 1864

Jones Thomas, weaver and parish clerk, Church street Resident in 1818

Jones William, agent to the Proprietors of the Park and Kettlebrook Collieries, Church street Resident in 1818

K

Keeling Elizabeth, straw bonnet maker, Church street Resident in 1818

Keeling James, plasterer and bricklayer, Lichfield street Resident in 1818

Keeling Joseph, plasterer and bricklayer, Lichfield street Resident in 1818

Keeling Joseph (Mr.), Aldergate street Resident in 1864

Keen Samuel, gardener, Lichfield street Resident in 1818

Keen Thomas, gardener, Gungate street Resident in 1818

(Continued from page 12)

Railways

The railways have given considerable animation to the place. Two lines run direct through the east end of the town - the Liverpool, Chester and Manchester line through the Trent Valley, and the Derby and Birmingham line of the Midland, intersecting and in close connection with those of the South and North Staffordshire lines - thus affording the greatest possible facility of travelling. The station is an exceedingly handsome building ; the, lower part is fitted up for the use of passengers by the Trent Valley line, and the upper compartments are used by the Derby and Birmingham company ; the latter line of railway crosses above the Trent Valley line at this point, and is then carried over a beautiful vale south-east of the town by a stupendous viaduct of nineteen lofty arches, on its route to Birmingham.

(Continued on page 18)

Kelly James (Rev.) Roman Catholic], Aldergate street Resident in 1864

Kendall Samuel, bricklayer, near Lichfield street Resident in 1818

Kendall Samuel, builder, Church street Resident in 1864

Kendrick (Mrs.), Cole hill Resident in 1864

Kerr Hannah (Mrs.), post mistress, Silver street Resident in 1818

Kesterton Thomas, cowkeeper, Aldergate street Resident in 1864

Kinson James, market gardener, Bolehall Resident in 1864

Kinson Rebecca (Mrs.), market gardener, Bolehall Resident in 1864

Kirkham Mary Ann (Miss), day school, Aldergate street Resident in 1864

Kitchen Clara & Jane (Misses), dressmakers, Gungate street Resident in 1864

Knight Joseph, farmer, Church street Resident in 1818

Knight William, boot and shoemaker, Silver street Resident in 1818

Knight William, bootmaker, Lichfield street Resident in 1864

Knight William esq., solicitor, Church street Resident in 1864

Knowles Amelia (Mrs.), Dog inn, Gungate street Resident in 1864

L

Lakin Anne, Straw hat maker, PLACGungateE street Resident in 1818

Lakin James, tailor, Bole bridge street Resident in 1818

Lakin William, watch & clock maker, Market street Resident in 1864

Langley Mary, (Mrs.), Shopkeeper, George street Resident in 1818

Langley Mrs., Gungate street Resident in 1864

Leary Frederick, commercial traveller, Cole hill Resident in 1864

Leaverisk Henry, schoolmaster, Lichfield street Resident in 1818

(Continued from page 17)

Serving the Population

In Tamworth is a library and reading room, under the patronage of Sir Robert Peel. There is a flourishing Savings bank. The whole parish contains 12,920 acres and had a population in 1861 of 10,190, of -whom 4,326 are in the borough of Tamworth.

(Continued on page 22)

Leigh Hen. Bluadell esq., Amington hall Resident in 1864

Lightwood John, schoolmaster, Church street Resident in 1818

Linford John, boot and shoemaker, Church street Resident in 1818

Littler William, grocer, Lichfield street Resident in 1864

Logan George, gardener, Gungate street Resident in 1864

Logan John, shopkeeper, Lichfield street Resident in 1864

Logan William Henry, brewer & wine & spirit merchant, George street Resident in 1864

Long Mary (Mrs.), Three Tuns, Lichfield street Resident in 1864

Lowe James, victualler, Recruiting Serjeant, Lichfield street Resident in 1818

Lowe James, boot and shoemaker, Peel's row Resident in 1818

Lucas Urram , victualler, Castle Inn, (excise office), Maket Street Resident in 1818

Lyon Jane (Mrs.), gentlewoman, Church street Resident in 1818

M

Machin Michael, boot and shoemaker, Market street Resident in 1818

Macne Norman, travelling draper, Aldergate street Resident in 1864

March William, blacksmith, near Lichfield street Resident in 1818

Markland John, fishing & all other net maker, Lichfield st Resident in 1864

Marklew Edward, butcher, Bolebridge street Resident in 1864

Marlow John, block printer, Church lane Resident in 18_8

Marriott John, gardener and seedsman, Eldergate street Resident in 1818

Marriott Mrs., Victoria road Resident in 1864

Marriott Thomas, gardener and seedsman, Gungate street Resident in 1818

Marshall George, boot and shoemaker and baker, Cole hill Resident in 1818

Marshall John, wood turner, Silver street Resident in 1864

Marshall Josiah, linen and wollen draper, gocer and agent to the Globe Fire Office, Cole hHill Resident in 1818

Marshall Thomas, bricklayer, builder and plasterer, Gungate street Resident in 1818

Massey Richard, papermaker, Lichfield street Resident in 1818

Matthews Adam, provision dealer & seedsman, Market st Resident in 1864

Matthews George, hatter & hosier, Church street Resident in 1864

Matthews Mr George, The Lees Resident in 1864

McLaren Mr. James, Albert road Resident in 1864

McTaggart James, manager National Provincial Bank of England, Market street. Resident in 1864

Mead John, govenor of the house of industry, Lady bridge bank Resident in 1818

Mee Sarah (Mrs.), milliner etc. Cole hill. Resident in 1864

Mercer William, saddler and harness maker, Market street Resident in 1818

Millington William, White Lion inn & Commercial hotel, & billiard rooms; Lichfield street Resident in 1864

Mills Mrs., Victoria road Resident in 1864

Mitchell Henry & Arthur, stonemasons, Aldergate street Resident in 1864

Mitchell Henry, stone and marble mason, Bole bridge street Resident in 1818

Mitchell James, hatter and hosier, Market street Resident in 1818

Montford Mary (Miss), young ladies' day & boarding school, Lady Bank house Resident in 1864

Moore Henry, turner and chair maker, George street Resident in 1818

Moore John, tailor, gigs and horses to hire, Lichfield street Resident in 1818

Moore Joseph, Bell inn, Gungate street Resident in 1864

Moore William, tailor, Lichfield street Resident in 1818

Morgan William, shopkeeper, Albert road Resident in 1864

Morrhall Joseph, beer retailer, Lichfield street. Resident in 1864

Mottram Henry, builder, Aldergate street Resident in 1864

Mould Rev. John, M.A.. [vicar], Cole hill Resident in 1864

Mountfort John, baker and flour dealer, Bole bridge street Resident in 1818

Mountfort Joseph, baker and flour dealer, Market street Resident in 1818

Myring Thomas, saddler & harness maker, Bolebridge street Resident in 1864

N

Naylor John, wheelwright, Bolebridge street Resident in 1864

Neal Sarah (Mrs.), milliner & dressmaker, Church street Resident in 1864

Nevill Richard esq., Bolebridge street Resident in 1864

Nevill Richard, solicitor; Bolebridge street Resident in 1864

Nevill Richard, schoolmaster, Bole bridge street Resident in 1818

Nevill Robert & Son, solicitors, George street Resident in 1864

Nevill Robert esq., George street Resident in 1864

Nevill Robert Wakley esq., George st Resident in 1864

Nevill Robert, solicitor, George street Resident in 1818

Newbold of Sale & Newbold, linen & woollen drapers, Market place Resident in 1864

Newbould Elizabeth, milliner and dress maker, Bole bridge street Resident in 1818

Newhold Richard, engraver to calico printers, Church street Resident in 1818

Nightingale Charles, victnaller, White Lion, Bole bridge street Resident in 1818

Nightingale William, tailor, Church street Resident in 1818

O

Oaks Charles, solicitor, Lichfield street Resident in 1818

Ordish John, farmer, Glascote Resident in 1864

Ordish John, sen. farmer, Amington green Resident in 1864

Ordish John; Jun, farmer, Amington green Resident in 1864

Ordish William, farmer, Glascote Resident in 1864

Oreton George, gardener, Greengate Resident in 1818

Orme John, chimney sweeper, Cole hill Resident in 1818

P

Pailett Thomas, boot & shoe maker, Lichfield street Resident in 1864

Pallett Edward, gardener, gungate street Resident in 1818

Palmer Fanry & Ann (Misses), dressmakers, Victoria road Resident in 1864

Palmer George, baker and flour dealer, Lichfield street Resident in 1818

Palmer Sarah shopkeeper, Cole hill Resident in 1818

Palmer Shirley, M.D., Eldergate street Resident in 1818

Parker Joseph, shopkeeper and brickmaker, Gungate street Resident in 1818

Parker Phillip beer retailer, Gungate street Resident in 1864

Parker Thomas, shoe warehouse, George street Resident in 1864

Parsons William, druggist, Market street Resident in 1818

Patrick Eliza (Mrs.), milliner, Aldergate street Resident in 1864

Patrick John, brick maker and malster, Church street Resident in 1818

Patrick Thomas, brickmaker, near Gungate street Resident in 1818

Patrick Thomas, gardener, & brick & tile maker, Brickhill hole Resident in 1864

Payne William, stay maker, tea dealer and grocer, George street Resident in 1818

Pecey Sarah (Miss), berlin wool repository, Cole hill Resident in 1864

Pegg James, clerk to Tamworth Friendly Institution, Bolebridge street Resident in 1864

Pegg James, beer retailer, Bolebridge street Resident in 1864

Pemberton Ann (Mrs.), beer retailer, George street Resident in 1864

Perrins & Harrison, coal owners & coal merchants, Kettlebrook wharf Resident in 1864

Perry Richard, Hare & Hounds, Lichfield street Resident in 1864

Peters Mr. George Storer, Bolebridge st Resident in 1864

Pimm Mr. Richard, Albert road Resident in 1864

Pimm Richard, baker, Market street Resident in 1864

Pipe John, grocer, Market street Resident in 1864

Pipe Miss, Church street Resident in 1864

Platts Henry, tarpaulin & rope maker, Lichfield street Resident in 1864

Platts Mrs., Aldergate street Resident in 1864

Pointon John, Old Boot, Lichfield street Resident in 1864

Powel Mr. Rees, Bolebridge street Resident in 1864

Prall Mr. Edward, Albert road Resident in 1864

Proudman Benjamin, shopkeeper, Cole hill Resident in 1864

Purden Thomas, saddler & harness maker, Silver street Resident in 1864

Peel Edmund, Esq., Bone hill and Lady bridge Bank Tamworth Resident in 1818

(Continued from page 18)

Borough

The Parliamentary borough consists of the old parish of Tamworth, and comprises all the townships round; of these Fazeley, Wilnecote and Wigginton are now district parishes, separated from Tamworth. In Amington, Hopwas, Bolehill, and Glascote there are chapels of ease. The parish registers are very old, and contain several instances of longevity, and some account of the movements of princes and armies. *(Continued on page 24)*

Peters Richard, currier and leather seller, Bole bridge street Resident in 1818

Pickard James, wollen and linen draper and grocer, Market street Resident in 1818

Pickard Joseph, College lane Resident in 1818

Pickering Thomas, turner and chair maker, Bole bridge street Resident in 1818

Pike Elizabeth, victualler,Jolly Button Turner, Bole bridge street Resident in 1818

Pipe Richard, grocer and druggist, Market place business address in 1818

Pipe Richard, Bone hill cottage Resident in 1818

R

Ramsell Eliza (Mrs.), hairdresser, Market street Resident in 1864

Rathbone William, glass and china dealer, black and whitesmith Market place Resident in 1818

Raybould Joseph, milliner & draper, Silver street Resident in 1864

Redfern Henry, engraver abd shopkeeper, Gungate street Resident in 1818

Redfern James, Joiner, Church lane Resident in 1818

Redfern Thomas, farmer, Amington Resident in 1864

Richardson James, gardener, Bolebridge street Resident in 1864

Richardson John, White Lion, Bolebridge street Resident in 1864
Richardson Joseph, gardener, Bolebridge street Resident in 1864

Richardson Thomas, gardener, Bolebridge street Resident in 1864

Riley John, joiner and wheelwright, Gungate street Resident in 1818

Riley Joseph, boot and shoemaker, Church street Resident in 1818

Robinson Louisa Caroline (Mrs.), Corn Exchange, Market place Resident in 1864

Robinson Mary, gentlewoman, Lichfield street Resident in 1818

Robinson William, vetinary surgeon, Lady bridge bank Resident in 1818

Robinson William, gardener and seedsman, Bole bridge street Resident in 1818

Robotham James, grocer and wool dealer, Cole hill Resident in 1818
Roby Mrs., Lady Bridge terrace Resident in 1864

Roby Thomas (senior), tanner, Cole hill Resident in 1818

Roby Thomas and son, tanner, Bole bridghe street Resident in 1818

Roe William, tailor and habit maker, Bole bridge street Resident in 1818

Roe William, tailor, Aldergate street Resident in 1864

Ruffe Frederic, chemist, George street Resident in 1864

Ruffe Mrs., Aldergate street Resident in 1864

S

Sadler Frederick & Alfred, druggists & grocers, Church st Resident in 1864

Sadler Henry, commercial traveller, Market place Resident in 1864

Sadler Mr. Frederick, Gungate street Resident in 1864

Sadler Richard, joiner and builder, Lichfield street Resident in 1818

Sadler Richard, carpenter, Hill cottage, Gungate street Resident in 1864

Sale & Newbold, linen & woollen drapers, Market place Resident in 1864

Salt Henry, Red Lion, Lichfield street Resident in 1864

Salt Philip, shopkeeper, Bole Bridge street Resident in 1818

Sanders George, Staffordshire Yeoman, Market place Resident in 1864

Sanders Joseph, higgler, Victoria road Resident in 1864

Sansom and Hunter, painters, plumbers and glaziers, Cole hill Resident in 1818

Saunders Joseph, blacksmith and farrier, Bole bridge street Resident in 1818

Saunders William, market gardener, Bolehall Resident in 1864

Saunders William, butcher, Bole bridge street Resident in 1818

Sergeant John, boot and shoemaker, Bole bridge street Resident in 1818

Sharp Deerham, gentleman, Lady bridge bank Resident in 1818

Sharpe Thomas, boot and shoemaker, Church lane Resident in 1818

Sharples Mrs., Lichfield street Resident in 1864

Sharples William esq., Lichfield st Resident in 1864

Sharples William, surgeon, Lichfield street Resident in 1864

Shaw John esq., Church street Resident in 1864

(Continued from page 22)

Fairs

The chartered fairs granted by Queen Elizabeth are held on the 4th May, 26th July, and 24th October, besides monthly Fairs of modern institution. They are now chiefly for the sale of cattle and. horses. The whole of the property is freehold.

(Continued on page 26)

Shaw John, solicitor, Church street Resident in 1864

Shenton Benjamin, auctioneer, Church street Resident in 1818

Shepherd Samuel, dyer, George street Resident in 1864

Sheppard Jacob, livery stable keeper & horse breaker, Aldergate street Resident in 1864

Shilcock John, victualler, Tamworth Arms, Market place Resident in 1818

Shilton Aaron, turner in brass and iron, Church street Resident in 1818

Shilton James, whitesmith and cutler, Market street Resident in 1818

Shorthouse Miss, Glascote Resident in 1864

Silk Charles, grocer, George street Resident in 1864

Simmons James, Gas Works Manager, Bolebridge street Resident in 1864

Skey George esq., J. P. Bone Hill lodge Resident in 1864

Slater Jesse, tailor, Bole bridge street Resident in 1818

Smedley Job, tinplate worker, Cole hill Resident in 1864

Smith E and M., milliners and dressmakers, Silver street Resident in 1818

Smith James, brazier and tin plate worker, George street Resident in 1818

Smith James, dealer in flour, bacon etc., George street Resident in 1818

Smith James, shopkeeper, Gungate street Resident in 1864

Smith Mercer esq., Bolehall Resident in 1864

Smith Mr. William, Glascote Resident in 1864

Smith Richard, shopkeeper, Lichfield street Resident in 1864

Smith Thomas, attorney's clerk, Lichfield street Resident in 1818

Sommers John, black and whitesmith, Eldergate street Resident in 1818

Spare Robert, cooper, Market street Resident in 1818

Spare Robert, metal dealer, Lichfield street Resident in 1864

Spencer William, beer retailer, Albert road Resident in 1864

Spooner Abraham, farmer, Royal's farm, Amington Resident in 1864

Spooner Mary, straw bonnet maker, Bole bridge street Resident in 1818

Spruce Samuel, manager of Glascote Colliery Company, coal owners, Glascote Resident in 1864

Spruce Samuel, mining engineer, Lichfield street Resident in 1864

Stamforth Josiah Wesley, commercial traveller, Lichfield st Resident in 1864

Starkey Charles. plumber &c. Lichfield street Resident in 1864

Starkey Charles, wheelwright, Aldergate street Resident in 1864

Starkey James, Coffee Pot, George street Resident in 1864

Starkie George, sawyer, Church lane Resident in 1818

Steer Miss, Spittals Resident in 1864

Stemson Robert, tailor & draper, George street Resident in 1864

Stevenson Rudland, tailor & draper, Market street Resident in 1864

Steverson Emily (Miss), straw bonnet maker, Market street Resident in 1864

Stretton George, grocer, Church street Resident in 1864

Stretton William, shopkeeper, Gungate street Resident in 1864

T

Taverner Mrs., Victoria road Resident in 1864

Taylor Thomas, boot & shoemaker, Amington Resident in 1864

Taylor William Garnett, jun. patent flax lint manufacturer, Castle mill Resident in 1864

Taylor William, carpenter, Lichfield street Resident in 1864

(Continued from page 24)

Church

The church of St. Editha is in good condition; it was formerly collegiate, and is a large noble structure; it had transepts, but there have been aisles, chancels, etc., added, destroying its cruciform appearance; its architecture is Gothic, but of different periods; there are two Norman arches in the centre of the church, where once stood the centre tower: the most curious object is the crypt under the south aisle nearly filled with human bones, collected chiefly, it is believed, from some battle field of the neighbourhood : a tesselated, (or tiled), pavement, found in the old churchyard, has been laid down in front of the communion table ; it also contains monuments of the Ferrers and other ancient families: the tower is square, surrounded by four octagonal turrets and spires; in one of the turrets is a double staircase of very curious construction. The date of the earliest register is 1558 The living is a vicarage, value £220, with residence: E.H. A. A'Court Repington, Esq., is the patron; the Rev. John Mould, M .A., of St. John's College, Cambridge, is rural dean and vicar ; the Rev. James Burdekin, curate, Rev: John Langton Gurney, curate, and Rev. Charles Jones, curate.

(Continued on page 27)

Tebbutt George, Railway tavern, George street Resident in 1864

Tempest William, Peel Arms inn, family hotel, commercial & posting house, Market street Resident in 1864

Temple John, currier and leather seller, Market street Resident in 1818

Temple Joseph, surveyor of taxes, Market street Resident in 1818

Tennant Phoebe (Mrs.), shopkeeper, Gungate street Resident in 1864

THEATRE , Gungate street Resident in 1818

Thirlby Widow, victualler boot, Lichfield street Resident in 1818

Thompson Mary (Mrs.), printer & bookseller, Market street Resident in 1864

Thompson Walter, sadler and harness maker, Church street Resident in 1818

Thornber John, shopkeeper, Bole bridge street Resident in 1818

Thurman Edward, plumber and galzier, glass and china dealer, George street Resident in 1818

Tillson Joseph. Old Stone Cross, Church street Resident in 1864

Tompson Mr. William John, George st Resident in 1864

Travis Rev. Elijah John, Aldergate st Resident in 1864

Tricklebank John, tailor, Church street Resident in 1864

Tromans Isaac, boiler & hurdle maker, round scuttle open pan & chain manufacturer, Amington boiler works Resident in 1864

Turner Mary (Mrs), lodging house, Victoria road Resident in 1864

Tylecote Samuel, wine and spirit merchant, and porter dealer, Cole hill Resident in 1818

Tyler Joseph, blacksmith, Gungate street Resident in 1864

(Continued from page 26)

Chapels

There are chapels for Independents, Wesleyans, Baptists and United Methodists; and also a Roman Catholic chapel, with a house belonging thereto. There are a Sunday and a National school, an infant school, and a Grammar school endowed by Queen Elizabeth. The number of scholars at the National and Sunday schools is very considerable.

(Continued on page 28)

Tyler William, blacksmith, Lichfield street Resident in 1818

U

Utermarck George esq., Lichfield st Resident in 1864

Uttermarck George, surgeon, Lichfield street Resident in 1864

V

Vale James, calico printer, Church street Resident in 1818

Vale Mrs., Church street Resident in 1864

Vaughton Joseph, boot and shoemaker, Cole street Resident in 1818

Vincent Joseph, butcher, George street Resident in 1818

Vinson Joseph, hairdresser, perfumer, dealer in hardware etc., Silver street Resident in 1818

W

Wain William, linen and woollen draper, wine and spirit merchant, ale and porter dealer and agent to the Birmingham Fire Office, George street Resident in 1818

Wakefield Thomas, Pretty Pigs, Amington Resident in 1864

Waldron James, painter, Gungate street Resident in 1864

Walker John, wine and spirit merchant and porter dealer, Market street Resident in 1818

Walker Thomas, Wheatsheaf, Church street Resident in 1864

(Continued from page 27)

County Court District
The following parishes and places comprise the county court district of Tamworth, and also the poor-law union:

Amington & Stonydelph,	Edingale,	Shuttington.
Austrey,	Fazeley,	Statfold,
Bolehall & Glascote,	Harlaston,	Tamworth,
Chilcote,	Hints,	Tamworth Castle,
Clifton	Kingsbury,	Thorpe
Campville,	Middleton,	Constantine,
Croxall,	Newton Regis,	Wigginton,
Canwell,	Scierscote,	Wilnecote.
Drayton Bassett,	Seekington,	

(Continued on page 30)

Wallis James, victualler, Three Tuns, Church street Resident in 1818

Wallis John, butcher, George street Resident in 1864

Walthew Thomas, blacksmith, Amington Resident in 1864

Walthew Thomas, Currier and leather seller, George street Resident in 1818

Walthew William, joiner and builder, Eldergate street Resident in 1818

Ward Rev. Michael, vicar of Lapley, Lichfield street Resident in 1818

Ward Richard, boot & shoe maker, Market street Resident in 1864

Ward Seth cooper, Eldergate street Resident in 1818

Ward Thomas, jun. glass & earthenware dealer, Lichfield st Resident in 1864

Warwick Frederick, Tweedale Arms & commercial house, close to Railway station, Victoria road Resident in 1864

Watterson Thomas, shoemaker, Market street Resident in 1818

Watton Samuel , nailor, Marshall's yard, Church street Resident in 1818

Watton Samuel, joiner and builder, Gungate street Resident in 1818

Watton Thomas, nail manufacturer, George street Resident in 1818

Watton Thomas, builder, Albert road Resident in 1864

Weatherhead Edward, shopkeeper, Church street Resident in 1864

Webb Thomas, boot and shoemaker, Market street Resident in 1818

Webb William, artist, Market street Resident in 1818

Webster Robert, boot and shoemaker, Church street Resident in 1818

Webster Thomas, blacksmith, Church street Resident in 1864

West Richard, painter and crier, Church street Resident in 1818

Weston John, grocer and calico printer, Bole bridge street Resident in 1818

Weston William, victualler, Bell Inn, George street Resident in 1818

White Thomas, brewer & maltster, Albert road Resident in 1864

Whitehouse and Hare, milliners and dress makers, Cole hill Resident in 1818

Whitehouse Charles, chimney sweeper, Gungate street Resident in 1864

Whitmore Mrs , Gungate street Resident in 1864

Whitmore Thomas, Park inn, Kettlebrook Resident in 1864

Whorrall William, land surveyor, Victoria road Resident in 1864

Whyman William, hairdresser, Bolebridge street Resident in 1864

Wilcox James, lime & coal agent, Aldergate street Resident in 1864

Wildman Thomas, Blacksmith, Lichfield street Resident in 1818

Wileman Samuel, spirit merchant, Market street Resident in 1864

Wiley Mrs., Gungate street Resident in 1864

Wilkinson Charles, tailor and draper, Church street Resident in 1818

Wilkius S, gardener, seedsman and carrier, Bole bridge street Resident in 1818

Willcox Charles, Cooper, Lichfield street Resident in 1818

Willcox James and sons, patten wood, tie and ring manufacturers and grocers, Lichfield street Resident in 1818

Willcox James , victualler and seedsman, White Lion Inn, Lichfield street Resident in 1818

Willcox John, butcher, Church street Resident in 1818

Willcox Samuel, print cutter, King street Resident in 1818

Willcox Thomas, hairdresser, Gungate street Resident in 1864

Willcox William, beer retailer, Aldergate street Resident in 1864

Willington Francis esq., Cole hill Resident in 1864

Willington & Argyle, solicitors, & clerks to trustees of Tamworth turnpike roads, Cole hill Resident in 1864

Wilson Peter, hairdresser, Church street Resident in 1864

Windridge Samuel, baker, Lichfield street Resident in 1864

(Continued from page 28)

HOPWAS is a pretty and compact little village, 2½ miles west from Tamworth, on the opposite side of the Tame, which is crossed by a handsome bridge, erected early in the present century. There is a Free school here, founded by Thomas Barnes in 1724, and endowed with land, etc., value about £20 per annum. There is a neat chapel here, in which the vicar and curates of Tamworth officiate. The population in 1861 was 277.

ALDER MILLS is a mile and a half west from Tamworth.

Coton is 2 miles north-west from Tamworth.

Tamworth Parish Clerk: William Boyes.

Withnall Thomas, victualler , Black Bull, George street Resident in 1818

Witllington Thomas, solicitor, Church street Resident in 1818
Wood James, shopkeeper, Gungate street Resident in 1864

Wood Joseph, basket maker, Lichfield street Resident in 1864

Wood William, haberdasher, Bolebridge street Resident in 1864

Woodcock Richard Ashmore, chemist, Market street Resident in 1864

Woodcock Richard, hair dresser and perfumer, Market street Resident in 1818

Woodcock Thomas, coach builder, Church street Resident in 1864

Woodhouse Frederick Augustus, wholesale clothier, Albert rd Resident in 1864

Woody John Francis esq., The Moat, Lichfield street Resident in 1864

Woody John Francis, surgeon, The Moat, Lichfield street Resident in 1864

Woody Robert Joham esq., The Moat Resident in 1864

Woody Robert, surgeon, Mont house, Lichfield street Resident in 1818

Woolley John Alfred, school teacher, Aldergate street Resident in 1864

Wootton John, tailor and draper, agent to the County Fire Office and constable of the Castle Liberty, George street Resident in 1818

Wootton William, butcher, George street Resident in 1818

Worrall William, boot & shoe maker, Bolebridge street Resident in 1864

Worthington John, victualler , Three Crowns, Lichfield street Resident in 1818

Wright James, gentleman, Lichfield street Resident in 1818

Wright John, joiner, Lady bridge bank Resident in 18_8

Wright Peter, Esq, Lichfield street Resident in 1818

Wriglesworth Richard, calico printer, Bole bridge street Resident in 1818

Y

Yarrow Alfred, hosier, hatter & outfitter, Market street & George street Resident in 1864

Young William, auctioneer and land surveyor and agent to the Commercial

www.ingramcontent.com/pod-product-compliance
Lightning Source LLC
Chambersburg PA
CBHW070845310526
45793CB00011B/583